CREATION'S VERY SELF

On the Personal Element in Recent Amerian Poetry

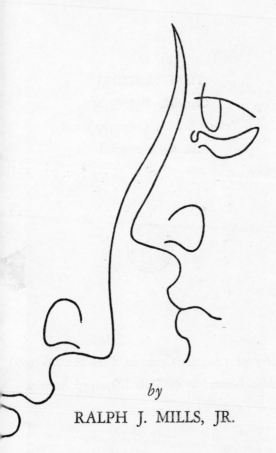

by

RALPH J. MILLS, JR.

With a Foreword by William Burford

PUBLISHED BY THE TEXAS CHRISTIAN UNIVERSITY PRESS

FIRST PRINTING

Copyright © 1969 by

Texas Christian University Press

Library of Congress Catalogue Card No. 76-86593

Manufactured in the United States of America

ACKNOWLEDGMENT is made to the following publishers for permission to reprint poems from the poets included in this essay: to Doubleday and Company for "Open House," "The Return," "Cuttings (Later)," "Praise to the End," "In a Dark Time," from *Collected Poems of Theodore Roethke;* City Lights Books for "The Day Lady Died," in *Lunch Poems* by Frank O'Hara, and "Above Pate Valley" in *Riprap and Cold Mountain Poems* by Gary Snyder; to Atheneum Publishers for "A Scale in May" from *The Moving Target* by W. S. Merwin; to Wesleyan University Press for "The Dream Flood" from *Drowning with Others* by James Dickey, for "The Morning Light" from *At the End of the Open Road* by Lewis Simpson, for "Confession to J. Edgar Hoover" from *Shall We Gather at the River* by James Wright; to Farrar, Straus & Giroux for "Grandparents," "Waking in the Blue" from *Near the Ocean* by Robert Lowell, for Dream Songs #8 and #29 from *77 Dream Songs* by John Berryman; to Houghton Mifflin Co. for "For the Year of the Insane" from *Live or Die* by Anne Sexton; to Harper and Row for "Getting There" from *Ariel* by Sylvia Plath; to New Directions Publishing Co. for "September 1961," "The Coming Fall" from *O Taste and See* by Denise Levertov, and "A Common Ground," from "Three Meditations" from *The Jacob's Ladder* by Denise Levertov; and to Gary Snyder for "Above Pate Valley" from *Riprap & Cold Mountain Poems.*

FOREWORD

The essay published here, "Creation's Very Self,"
was read by Mr. Mills on May 7, 1969, on the occasion
of the annual Cecil Williams Lecture in American
Literature at Texas Christian University. The lecture-
ship for 1969 was part of a larger occasion celebrat-
ing creativity in contemporary American poetry, painting, and architecture, and the English Department of
the University was most happy to be able also to present Denise Levertov, the poet, whose work has a
leading place in Mr. Mills's picture of the present
poetic scene. In addition, the Department invited Mr.
Paul Rudolph, the architect, and the Directors of the
three Fort Worth museums (one still in the making
—the Kimbell Museum) to participate in the various
activities connected with the two day occasion—Dr.
Richard Brown, Mr. Harry Hopkins, and Mr. Mitchell
Wilder. "Creation's Very Self," Mr. Mills's tribute to
the accomplishments of the most recent American
poetry, was the opening event of the two days.

As Mr. Mills has described it, the movement of
modern American poetry has been towards a dramatization of the poet's intimate psychological self, a

profoundly interior exploration, as if the only ultimate honesty could be found there. Poetry has thus attempted to follow a path that the novel took before it—surely, in terms of psychological depth one would go to Dostoevsky or Proust or even Conrad, rather than to the poets roughly contemporaneous with such novelists. After Shakespeare no poet in the English language is really read, it seems to me, for psychological content, when compared to the English and American novelists. An objection might be raised that Emily Dickinson, for example, wrote a powerful and exacting poetry of the inner self, in a meditative tradition whose roots are in the English metaphysicals. But at once what a difference we feel between this poetic intensity directed upon a quite recognizable and, in truth, expected Christian version of the self's history— what a difference between this and the tangle Faulkner enters when he works into his characters' lives, though Faulkner has certain Christian guideposts by which he sometimes takes his bearings.

From this viewpoint of the relatively much greater psychological interest of the novel over poetry—if we can accept such a comparison, for it may well be that we have quite different expectations in reading poetry from those we have in reading the novel—the poems of Eliot, once considered revolutionary, can now be seen as familiar and rather attenuated versions of a self which Saint Augustine in his *Confessions* expressed with the force of an original psychological discovery, an exploratory thrust into new regions. And beside the explorations of several of the poets whom Mr. Mills describes in this essay, we can hardly believe any more that Eliot was an explorer, to take his own word for his idea of the poet in *Four Qaurtets*. Eliot's presentation of the human self, his own and all men's, was bound to the essential Christian drama of the self which Augustine drew the plot of at the beginning of Christian literature. Now, if we believe in constants, then, of course, this drama is forever valid, forever renewable, and may have again and again the force of its original, or at least nearly so. If we do not believe in constants, and then set out or are driven to look at the self all over again, whether it be an abyss in Yeats's word, implying darkness and the unknown, or illuminated with lights not yet registered in the Christian or Dantean spectrum of judgment—then we have something like the feeling, I think, which Mr. Mills has so sympathetically suggested in this essay.

But—there *may be* constants, and if so, then much of what Mr. Mills calls modern confessional poetry—confessional in a very different sense from Augustine or Eliot—might in the long run appear as a kind of psychological indulgence or irrelevance. The possibility should, perhaps, not be raised from a historical viewpoint, for who knows what version of the human self may prevail, or be convincing. Perhaps each version is given its time. The test may best be faced, after all, in the meeting between the reader's self and the poet's poem in each particular instance, in the intimacy which as Mr. Mills has pointed out is the kind of contact the typical modern poem asks for. Of what is the self made, of what are different kinds of selves made—this is the pressing concern of the most prevalent American poem of the immediate time.

WILLIAM BURFORD

CREATION'S VERY SELF

On the Personal Element in Recent American Poetry

Categories and classifications are among the de-humanizing evils of our time. Almost anywhere we turn in these bleak, disordered days of recent history there lies in wait one kind of mechanism or other which has as its end the obscuration or destruction of what is unique and particular, unmistakably itself: the very identity of a person, an experience, an object. Since nothing keeps alive our awareness of the concrete and specific more than poetry, it is the worst sort of folly to force it into convenient patterns or make it demonstrate some invented principle. Such efforts are nets to catch the wind, a wind which has sacred sources because it is the Muse's or the spirit's motion, or, following Charles Olson's definition of the poetic line, because it is "the breathing of the man who writes, at the moment that he writes."[1] In spite of every attempt to do something with or to it, as W. H. Auden says in his elegy for Yeats, poetry "survives,/A way of happening, a mouth." And so it should be. The few distinctions and delineations that I make, then, in what follows are loose, not rigid, and are designed for the exigencies of the occasion. My purpose here will be neither that of the scholar nor the theorist, but, if you will, that of the enthusiast-commentator who wishes to bring to your attention some contemporary poets and their poems, to remark certain qualities that seem prominent and characteristic, and to disappear, leaving you, I hope, with a desire to know recent poetry better.

One distinction I think necessary to draw before we can talk about current writing separates *modernist* poetry from *contemporary* poetry. I shall presume that the modernist poets are those whose names spring first to mind when we think of poetry in this century, the pioneer figures such as Yeats, Eliot, Pound, Stevens, W. C. Williams, Marianne Moore, most of them born a decade or more before the turn of the century and all but a few now dead. These modernists have in common the fact that each of them, in his or her own way, participated in that poetic revolution which cast aside the vestiges of Victorianism and outworn literary conventions, infused new vigor into diction and rhythm, disclosed new possibilities of form, and brought poetry into meaningful relationship with the actualities of modern life—a relationship which is being renewed by poets today. Having accomplished all this, the modernist poets proceeded into the years of their maturity and produced some of their greatest work long after that revolutionary movement of what Randall Jarrell once called "irregularly cooperative experimentalism"[2] was over. So, in a period that ostensibly belonged to their successors, those poets who are the first of the ones I shall call contemporaries, we find extraordinary achievements such as Eliot's *Four Quartets,* Pound's later *Cantos,* Williams' *Paterson,* and Stevens' *The Auroras of Autumn* looming intimidatingly over the poetic landscape.

What separates the contemporaries from the modernists, to begin with, is the simple fact of being born too late to join in that radical movement which, beginning around 1910, overthrew reigning literary modes and aesthetic tastes, and with increasing help from literary critics, itself solidified into an establishment. Not only did these younger poets emerge in the wake of a full-scale artistic revolution, whose chief participants were still around and still quite productive, but they were confronted with new versions of the literary past and a variety of prospects for using it which Eliot's notion of tradition, the practice of his poetry, and an expanding body of literary criticism made available. The liberating influence of William Carlos Williams was yet to be felt.

So it was that Stanley Kunitz, Richard Eberhart, Theodore Roethke, John Berryman, Robert Lowell, Karl Shapiro, and others who began to write in the decade of the 1930's, had to seek their own voices, searching them out through the arduous process of trying on and discarding models, guides, and influences from the poetic tradition and from modernist writers alike, without the benefit of any shared aesthetic principle or revolutionary artistic purpose. They did have in common a dogged attentiveness to the inner necessities of imaginative vision and to the difficult struggle for style. In this situation there were both burdens and blessings. If these poets, and many others who followed them in the late 1940's and the 1950's, felt overshadowed by most of their elders and confined by what Donald Hall terms a critical "orthodoxy" that required "a poetry of symmetry, intellect, irony, and wit,"[3] they were freed as individuals from the demands made by literary movements to an energetic and single-minded concentration on the making of poems, a concentration that brought, in due time, Roethke in *The Lost Son,* Lowell in *Life Studies,* Berryman in *Homage to Mistress Bradstreet,* and Shapiro in *The Bourgeois Poet,* for example, to the kind of poetic breakthrough James Dickey calls "The Second Birth"—an intense imaginative liberation, achieved at great personal cost, in which the poet, like a snake shedding his dead skin, frees himself of the weight of imposed styles and current critical criteria to come into the place of his own authentic speech. The secret of this renewal, Dickey observes, "does not, of course, reside in a complete originality, which does not and could not exist. It dwells, rather, in the development of personality, with its unique weight of experience and memory, as a writing instrument, and in the ability to give literary influence a new dimension which has the quality of this personality as informing principle. The Second Birth is largely a matter of self-criticism and endless experiment, presided over by an unwavering effort to ascertain what is most satisfying to the poet's self as it develops, or as it remains more clearly what it has always been."[4]

It is precisely here, with Dickey's notion of the poet's personality "as informing principle," that I want to note an important difference between the critical views derived from the modernist movement and the practice of contemporaries: a difference that has been heightened in the last decade and a half by the appearance of the Beat poets, the Projectivists, the confessional poets, and what is often called a new Surrealism or poetry of the unconscious. I have used in my title the term "personal element," which is purposely more general than Dickey's "personality," so it might apply equally to the work of a number of poets who have differing aims and emphases; but both terms oppose the view handed down from Eliot and the New Criticism that poetry and the emotions it conveys are, or should be, impersonal, and that an author's personality and life are to be excluded from his writings. In many of their poems Eliot, Pound, Stevens, and others, stress the poet's anonymity by employing fictional masks, invented speakers or *personae,* thus enforcing a division between writer and work. The original motive for such objectivity seems genuine enough: to rid poetry of biographical excesses and the residue of

4

the Romantics' preoccupation with personality which had seduced attention from the true object of interest, the poem itself. Eliot, in his famous essay of 1917, "Tradition and the Individual Talent," declares that "the more perfect the artist, the more completely separate in him will be the man who suffers and the mind which creates;" and again he says, "The progress of the artist is a continual self-sacrifice, a continual extinction of personality."[5] While it cannot be gone into here, much of what Eliot says has great value and will continue to speak to later generations. But the emphasis on the poet as an impersonal or anonymous "medium" passed out of Eliot's essay to become an important part of the critical atmosphere; consequently the poem came to be considered a neutral object, a vessel filled with the feelings of nobody, what Louis Simpson names "the so-called 'well-made' poem that lends itself to the little knives and formaldehyde of a graduate school."[6]

Among the pioneer modernists William Carlos Williams, with his anti-academicism, interest in the immediacies of experience and the spoken language, and sense of the singularity of form in the poem, and William Butler Yeats, with his insistence on the poet's creation of his personality, his anti-self, stand out in marked contrast to Eliot. The decidedly personal character of Yeats' voice, growing bolder and more idiosyncratic as his career lengthened out, could serve as a masterly example for Roethke, Kunitz, Lowell, Berryman, and other contemporary poets in quest of a personal idiom, a speech vibrating with their lives. Writing in his autobiographies of what he saw in Dante and Villon, the Irish poet might have been describing the figure he makes in his own poems. "Such masters," he says, "would not, when they speak through their art, change their luck; yet they are mirrored in all the suffering of desire. The two halves of their nature are so completely joined that they seem

5

to labour for their objects, and yet to desire whatever happens, being at the same time predestinate and free, creation's very self. We gaze at such men in awe, because we gaze not at a work of art, but at the re-creation of the man through that art . . ."[7]

Contemporary poets, then, with a few forerunners providing guidance, begin to cultivate their own inwardness as material for poetry or to look to the immediacies of their own situation for valid experience. In reaction to impersonality and rationalism, critical prescription and dissection, they seek a personal mode of utterance to embody perceivings and intuitions very much their own. As Robert Creeley comments, "Confronting such *rule* [ie. a critical rule of rationality and taste], men were driven back upon the particulars of their own experience, the literal *things* of an immediate environment, wherewith to acknowledge the possibilities of their own lives."[8] With rare exceptions like Robert Duncan, subjective experience no longer is translated into the kind of larger symbolic or metaphysical frameworks sustained by some of the modernists. Contemporary poets give the impression of beginning their poems nearer the brink of private intuition and feeling, and of trying, for the sake of authentic testimony, to remain as close to it as they are able. Nor do these poets hesitate to speak in their poems as themselves, for the individual voice is likewise to be understood as a sign of authenticity. In general, there is a distrust among contemporaries of systematizing; those who have known some sort of visionary or mystical experience—Roethke or Eberhart, say—refuse to acc⌒unt for it by intellectual means or to locate it within some comprehensive explanation of things. Instead, these experiences are enclosed in the heart of the poems which sprang from them; as a result, they are not divisible from the selves to whom they occurred.

6

Contemporary poets might take one of their chief mottoes from Wordsworth, who, in the preface to the *Lyrical Ballads* of 1800, after asking himself "what is a Poet?" and "To whom does he address himself?" answers unequivocally, "He is a man speaking to men." And we can add to this statement—thinking not only of Lowell, Eberhart or Roethke but of more recent poets, of Anne Sexton or John Logan, Gary Snyder or Frank O'Hara, Denise Levertov or William Stafford—that each poet wishes to speak to us, without impediment, from the deep center of a personal engagement with existence. For the contemporary poet enters into himself and the particulars of his experience in order to bring into being in his work that true poetic "self which [he] is waiting to be," to borrow a phrase from Ortega y Gassett[9] that confirms Yeats' remarks. The activity in which he engages is not just the construction of objects but the fashioning of a language that will ultimately awaken and transform the inner world of his readers. We approach here Martin Buber's description of "the primary word *I—Thou*" which "can be spoken only with the full being." The artist who creates, in Buber's thought, "may withhold nothing of himself."[10] So, for our contemporaries, we can perhaps say that poetic creation moves toward an intimacy, a communion of selves made available to the reader, if he will assume his part in it, through the agency of the unique poetic self we encounter speaking to us there. The contemporary poem requires dialogue to fulfill itself; once received, it inhabits us, unfolds a space within where we meet another presence, the poet's, through the order and resonance of words and images he has formed. "So," Kenneth Rexroth can rightly say, "speech approaches in poetry not only the directness and the impact but the unlimited potential of act."[11]

Recent American poetry, with its chosen precursors in Whitman, Williams, Pound, Hart Crane, and the writing of European and Latin American poets influenced by Surrealism and Expressionism, as well as Chinese and Japanese verse, discards artificial barriers that put distance between poet, poem, and reader; searches out new kinds of informality in the attempt to be more congruent with the shapes of experience. The contemporary poet recreates himself as a personality, an identifiable self within his poetry, that is, of course, a self who has been selected and heightened in the process, captured in essence, and so is not perhaps a full likeness of the author as a physical, workaday person outside the poem yet could not be mistaken for someone else. As we read the poems of our contemporaries, we recognize a certain magnanimous gesture in their acts of creation, a profoundly touching and human gesture through which the poet voluntarily stands exposed as "creation's very self" before us. In an age in which inner disorientation occurs because the individual's acts and thoughts appear to have no issue bearing his stamp but are swallowed by the vast technical apparatus of social, economic, and political forces that comprise our monolithic city-states the poet invites us to share his pursuit of identity; to witness the dramatization of the daily events of his experience —so closely resembling our own; to be haunted by the imagery of his dreams or the flowing stream of his consciousness; to eavesdrop on relationships with friends and lovers; to absorb the shock of his deep-seated fears and neuroses, even mental instability and madness, and through them to realize the torments of our time; and finally to reach with him that redeeming state of what Denise Levertov calls "Attention," which is no less than "the *exercise* of Reverence for the 'other forms of life that want to live.'"[12]

For the rest, let us see, in the abbreviated manner imposed by our limitations, some specific instances of the personal element in several poets and kinds of poetry of the last three decades. My first choice is Theodore Roethke, who died prematurely at the height of his powers in 1963. He produced work of such high quality that I feel sure he must be ranked as one of the finest American lyric poets. Appropriately enough for our subject, too, the pattern of his writing demonstrates in advance of many of his contemporaries the trying process of a "Second Birth," after an earlier period which merely hints at the penetrating experience he has yet to realize. The poems of his first collection, *Open House* (1941), show fundamental gifts: a fine ear, close acquaintance with the natural world, a good sense of language; but in spite of worthy pieces one feels that there remain all sorts of resources and energies still to be tapped. The declarations of the title poem support this feeling:

> My truths are all foreknown,
> This anguish self-revealed.
> I'm naked to the bone
> With nakedness my shield.
> Myself is what I wear:
> I keep the spirit spare.

"Myself is what I wear"—the announcement might have been made somewhere in *Leaves of Grass;* however, Roethke has not quite earned the right to say this. In the next half dozen years he broke through, in the so-called Greenhouse poems, to those deeper layers of himself that would draw him on to the radical experimentation of "The Lost Son" and the subsequent poems of his childhood sequence. Commenting on this quoted passage three decades later, and only a few months before his death, Roethke remarks:

> This poem is a clumsy, innocent, desperate asseveration. I am not speaking of the empirical self, the flesh-bound ego; it's a single word: *myself,* the aggregate of the several selves, if you will. The spirit or soul—should we say the self, once perceived, *becomes* the soul?—this I was keeping "spare" in my desire for the essential. But the spirit need not be spare: it can grow gracefully and beautifully like a tendril, like a flower.[13]

With the 1940's Roethke started shattering the restraints upon his previous work, pressing beyond the surfaces of experience toward the hidden sources. What he began to discover was, of course, himself, or those "several selves" he mentions, through a return in memory and imagination to his childhood, his family's floral establishment with its huge greenhouses and the acreage of woods and fields beyond, his uncle's suicide and his Prussian father's death from cancer when the poet was just fifteen.[14] This return to the past, which was simultaneously a descent into himself, could prove agonizing, if poetically rewarding, as he says in his poem "The Return:"

> A cold key let me in
> That self-infected lair;
> And I lay down with my life,
> With the rags and rotting clothes,
> With a stump of scraggy fang
> Bared for a hunter's boot.

But past experience which came alive then in his imagination finds a language that carries it to the page with the urgency and sensuous immediacy of life itself. At first, Roethke scrutinizes the lives of flowers and plants, even the tiny insects inhabiting their leaves. Yet he does not render this "vegetable realm" completely by itself; everywhere the presence of the poet, both as child-observer (since the poems draw upon vivid memories) and imaginative participant, can be felt, however obliquely. In "Cuttings (Later)" he claims his affinity with this world: the struggling into life visible there parallels his efforts to renew and complete himself:

> I can hear, underground, that sucking and sobbing,
> In my veins, in my bones, I feel it,—
> The small waters seeping upward,
> The tight grains parting at last.
> When sprouts break out,
> Slippery as fish,
> I quail, lean to beginnings, sheath-wet.

The childhood sequence opening with "The Lost Son," which takes a poetic leap beyond the greenhouse pieces, dramatizes what is now Roethke's imaginative preoccupation—the evolution of the self.

Through daring formal combinations, these poems convey a direct apprehension of inner and outer experience, the progressions and reversals of psychic life as the self seeks identity and spiritual reality. Beginning with early years, they proceed through adolescence, the torments of sexuality, the loss of the father, and on toward phases of illumination in which the self attains to an ecstatic, mystical communion with the surrounding animate and inanimate cosmos. Though Roethke indicates that the anonymous protagonist of these poems is meant to serve as a universal figure or everyman, both biographical detail and the intensity of the poetic experience reveal the poet's personal involvement with the speaker, whose consciousness is realized in all its complexity through an impressive array of poetic devices. He lists their "ancestors" as "German and English folk literature, particularly Mother Goose; Elizabethan and Jacobean drama, especially the songs and rants; the Bible; Blake and Traherne; Dürer."[15] In these poems Roethke avoids at all costs the intervention of explanation, interpretation, or judgment; as readers, we are compelled to live through the experience of the self, its sufferings and joys, conveyed directly, until we recognize that it is both the poet's and our own. Roethke also brings us to what technological man has forgotten, the inmost being of things, the essential life we share with creation:

> Arch of air, my heart's original knock,
> I'm awake all over:
> I've crawled from the mire, alert as a saint or a dog;
> I know the back-stream's joy, and the stone's eternal
>   pulseless longing.
> Felicity I cannot hoard.
> My friend, the rat in the wall, brings me the
>   clearest messages;
> I bask in the bower of change;
> The plants wave me in, and the summer apples;
> My palm-sweat flashes gold;
> Many astounds before, I lost my identity to a
>   pebble;
> The minnows love me, and the humped and
>   spitting creatures.
>
> (From Praise to the End!)

In his love poems and later meditative pieces and metaphysical lyrics Roethke continues his relentless pursuit of personal unity of being through the relation of self to the beloved, to the cosmos, and finally to God. Some of the last poems, written with an awareness of approaching death, disclose that solitary confrontation with the Divine which becomes an excruciating course of self-annihilation before it turns into the mystical union at the very boundaries of human life. My example is "In a Dark Time," the initial poem of *Sequence, Sometimes Metaphysical:*

> In a dark time, the eye begins to see,
> I meet my shadow in the deepening shade;
> I hear my echo in the echoing wood—
> A lord of nature weeping to a tree.
> I live between the heron and the wren,
> Beasts of the hill and serpents of the den.
> What's madness but nobility of soul
> At odds with circumstance? The day's on fire!
> I know the purity of pure despair,
> My shadow pinned against a sweating wall.
> That place among the rocks—is it a cave,
> Or winding path? The edge is what I have.
> A steady storm of correspondences!
> A night flowing with birds, a ragged moon,
> And in broad day the midnight come again!
> A man goes far to find out what he is—
> Death of the self in a long, tearless night,
> All natural shapes blazing unnatural light.
> Dark, dark my light, and darker my desire.
> My soul, like some heat-maddened summer fly,
> Keeps buzzing at the sill. Which I is *I*?
> A fallen man, I climb out of my fear.
> The mind enters itself, and God the mind,
> And one is One, free in the tearing wind.

While our limitations do not permit detailed comment,[16] let us anyway recognize in the poem an archetypal pattern of death and rebirth, of descent by the poet into his own nature, there to confront its confusions, complexities, and impurities personified in the figure of his "shadow" or double and to learn the agony of being parted from that in himself which must be abandoned—through a type of ritual or symbolic dying to oneself—if he is to achieve renewal in

12

the form of communion with God, a communion that is likewise a moment of self-integration or unity of being. The poem gathers strength from the oppositions and perils of spiritual quest, but these qualities would not impress us were it not for the feeling of the poet's individual involvement with them. To be sure, the imagery and thematic design of the poem evoke abundant associations from various traditions of religious thought; yet it is when we grasp these meanings as essential portions of a lived experience which is the poet's that they speak with conviction, the conviction born of personal witness. Roethke, in a symposium, says of the poem that it was "dictated . . . something given, scarcely mine at all. For about three days before its writing I felt disembodied, out of time; then the poem virtually wrote itself, on a day in summer, 1958."[17] The phrase "scarcely mine at all" does not, once we think of it in the context of the specific poem, contradict what I have been saying by separating the poet from his work. Rather, it points to an unusually heightened subjectivity, articulated in its totality from those regions of inwardness where it was prepared in secret. Roethke might also have commented on this poem, as on all of his poetry, with Whitman's words from "Song of Myself:" "I am the man, I suffer'd, I was there . . ."

Glancing around the current literary scene, we observe a number of younger poets who in certain ways fall in a line of descent from Roethke, though I should say at once that I am not speaking of direct imitation or stylistic influence. Rather, I am thinking of those poets who, however different from one another (and these differences are frequently considerable), create a poetry which depends heavily upon intuitive association, dream, the pre-conscious and the unconscious; a poetry highly responsive to the techniques of modern European writing; a poetry which proceeds by "a logic of the imagination" rather than "a logic of concepts," to borrow Eliot's distinction with respect to St.-John

13

Perse.[18] Whether treating in some form or other the fusion of outer and inner life, as, say, in various poems by Frank O'Hara, David Ignatow, William Stafford, and John Logan; entering into the being of other creatures or men by an imaginative extension, as in James Dickey's writing; giving voice to the hidden dream life of America, as some of the poems by Robert Bly, Louis Simpson, and James Wright do; or fashioning a rich but hermetic language of association and evocation, like W. S. Merwin's, this poetry discloses its highly personal character. For in each instance the poet, tired of the betrayal of his deepest feelings and most significant experiences by attempting to force them into conventional forms, tired of the intrusion of intellect and reason (Roethke called the latter "That dreary shed, that hutch for grubby schoolboys!" and countered, "The hedgewren's song says something else.")[19] upon the free exercise of imagination, tired of the arid critical formulations of the academies, has moved in the direction of the illogical and irrational, the private and intimate. Louis Simpson calls this tendency Surrealist, though he clearly disavows any identification with the rigid theories and dogmas proposed by André Breton. In a recent anthology he writes:

> The next step—it is already occurring—is to reveal the movements of the subconscious. The Surrealist poet—rejecting on the one hand the clichés of the rational mind, and on the other, a mere projection of irrational images—will reveal the drama and narrative of the subconscious. The images move, with the logic of dreams.[20]

We know at once from this statement that Simpson does not wish merely to revive the Surrealist practice of automatic writing. In a later article he insists that "poetry represents not unreason but the total mind, including both reason and unreason,"[21] by which he perhaps means the shaping powers of the conscious mind at work upon the materials provided by the subconscious. The French Surrealist poet Paul Eluard, who *is* convinced of the value of automatic writing,

14

has a passage which is helpful in clarifying differences between dream and poem, the images issuing from below consciousness and the impressions and sensations which continue to come from without. In spite of certain discrepancies between Simpson's and Eluard's statements, both aim at a new fusion of interior and exterior experience which will result in radically altered poetic imagery. Eluard says:

> You don't take the story of a dream for a poem. Both are living reality, but the first is a memory, immediately altered and transformed, an adventure, and of the second nothing is lost, nothing is changed. The poem desensitizes the universe to the advantage of human faculties, permits man to see differently other things. His former vision is dead, or false. He discovers a new world, he becomes a new man.
>
> People have thought that automatic writing makes poems useless. On the contrary! It increases or develops the domain of examination of poetic awareness, by enriching it. If awareness is perfect, the elements which automatic writing draws from the inner world and the elements of the outer world are balanced. Thus made equal, they mingle and merge in order to form poetic unity.[22]

By whatever methods they proceed, the poets I am grouping loosely here tend to create work that moves with "the logic of dreams," to repeat Louis Simpson's phrase, or to achieve a transformation of outer reality through its assimilation to the inward self. Unlike Roethke, who had no talent for languages, they have been engaged in a good deal of translating, as well as reading, of foreign poets. While it is not, as a rule, easy to indicate with assurance the influence of one poet upon another, familiarity with important modern poets from other countries, among them Neruda, Lorca, Vallejo, Char, Bonnefoy, Michaux, Trakl, Rilke, Benn, Mayakovsky, Pasternak, and Voznesensky, has helped to liberate American poetry from logic and wit, "epithets and opinions."[23]

Let me offer, at this point, a brief anthology of poetic effects deriving from these tendencies, and

15

offer it with some but not too much comment, since such poetry, coming as it does from the "total mind" of the poet, needs first to be taken in by the reader's or listener's "total mind."

In the poems of the late Frank O'Hara, whose accidental death at the age of forty cut off a great talent, there is considerable variety but also, in the end, a unity of impression. Like his friend Kenneth Koch, he gives the reader a sense of being talked to, rather than simply overheard. A voice addresses us, or someone of the poet's acquaintance whose person we inhabit while reading the poem; this voice may be gay, breezy, and whimsical, it may be elegaic or remorseful, tender and erotic, or it may pour forth in a rich jumble the contents of the poet's consciousness in its ceaseless flow. As is often noted, O'Hara has close affinities with contemporary painters, especially those named Abstract Expressionists or the New York action painters: Jackson Pollock, Franz Kline, Willem de Kooning, Philip Guston, and others. Pollock, in a written statement, tells why he prefers his canvases laid out on the floor rather than on easel or wall: "I feel nearer, more a part of the painting, since this way I can walk around it, work from the four sides, and literally be *in* the painting."[24] These remarks apply equally to O'Hara, in whose poems the poet's self is very evident, moving about freely, uninhibited by rules, concerned only with the realization of personal experience in language. "What is happening to me, allowing for lies and exaggerations which I try to avoid, goes into my poems," he explains in a statement on his poetics. "I don't think my experiences are clarified or made beautiful for myself or anyone else, they are just there in whatever form I can find them."[25] That form is the unpredictable, unliterary but very poetic form of life itself. The poem "The Day Lady Died" begins with the rather trivial events surrounding O'Hara's preparations for a weekend out

16

of New York visiting friends; almost at the poem's conclusion, along with two cartons of cigarettes, he casually buys a newspaper and there reads of the death of the great jazz singer, Billie Holliday. In the closing lines a memory of her singing overwhelms him as the original occasion did, though now her death leaves him with only that recollection:

It is 12:20 in New York a Friday
three days after Bastille day, yes
it is 1959 and I go get a shoeshine
because I will get off the 4:19 in Easthampton
at 7:15 and then go straight to dinner
and I don't know the people who will feed me
I walk up the muggy street beginning to sun
and have a hamburger and a malted and buy
an ugly NEW WORLD WRITING to see what the
poets in Ghana are doing these days
                          I go to the bank
and Miss Stillwagon (first name Linda I once heard)
doesn't even look up my balance for once in her life
and in the GOLDEN GRIFFIN I get a little
    Verlaine
for Patsy with drawings by Bonnard although I do
think of Hesiod, trans. Richard Lattimore or
Brendhan Behan's new play or *Le Balcon* or *Les
    Nègres*
of Genet, but I don't, I stick with Verlaine
after practically going to sleep with quandariness
and for Mike I just stroll into the PARK LANE
Liquor Store and ask for a bottle of Strega and
then I go back where I came from to 6th Avenue
and the tobacconist in the Ziegfield Theatre and
casually ask for a carton of Gauloises and a carton
of Picayaunes, and a NEW YORK POST with her
    face on it
and I am sweating a lot by now and thinking of
leaning on the john door in the 5 SPOT
while she whispered a song along the keyboard
to Mal Weldron and everyone and I stopped
    breathing

By way of contrast with the disarming openness of O'Hara's approach, a few stanzas from W. S. Merwin's "A Scale in May" suggest the poet's embarkation on a trying interior journey, frightening in its solitude and its challenge, for the goal is some honest understanding of existence, which is always

17

threatened by death and nothingness. Traveling light, Merwin takes with him only the possibility of poetry and a resolute integrity. The subjective nature of the poem's statements, their division into separate sections of three lines, each having the quality of a gnomic utterance, lead us to believe we have, by chance, come upon the poet in profound conversation with himself and are trespassers of his inner world. But that is not really the case. Once we begin to listen to what he is saying, its strange obliquity becomes evocative; its indefiniteness belongs to the elusive nature of spiritual quests. Then we cross over into that world, which he has so beautifully realized through what he calls "the great language itself, the vernacular of the imagination:"[26]

> Now all my teachers are dead except silence
> I am trying to read what the five poplars are writing
> On the void
>
> Of all the beasts to man alone death brings justice
> But I desire
> To kneel in the doorway empty except for the song
>
> Who made time provided also its fools
> Strapped in watches and with ballots for their choices
> Crossing the frontiers of invisible kingdoms
>
> To succeed consider what is as though it were past
> Deem yourself inevitable and take credit for it
> If you find you no longer believe enlarge the temple
>
> Through the day the nameless stars kept passing the door
> That have come all that way out of death
> Without questions

In a note written for the dust jacket of his collection *Drowning with Others* (1962) James Dickey declares, "my subject matter is inevitably my own life, my own obsessions, possessions and renunciations;" and later adds, "In these poems I have tried to come into that place in myself which is mine." One of the features of Dickey's poetry is a power of imagination that enables him to feel the essential being of others as if it were his own, to be haunted by the living and

18

the dead, and by an animistic universe. Ordinary objects, situations, patterns of nature in his poems suddenly assume the conformations of myth or join in rituals of initiation and transformation, interchanging identities, and progressing toward transcendent revelations. Here, to be specific, are the opening lines of "The Dream Flood," where imaginative re-enactment of archetypal details in a fluid, magical cosmos provides the aspect of personal myth:

> I ask and receive
> The secret of falling unharmed
> Forty nights from the darkness of Heaven,
> Coming down in sheets and in atoms
> Until I descend to the moon
> Where it lies on the ground
> And finds in its surface the shining
> It knew it must have in the end.
> No longer increasing, I stand
> Taking sunlight transmitted by stone,
> And then begin over fields
> To expand like a mind seeking truth . . .

Less cosmic in its proportions, Louis Simpson's brief poem "The Morning Light" projects through just a few suggestive images those private associations by means of which the imagination quickens a sense of our private lives or destinies:

> In the morning light a line
> Stretches forever. There my unlived life
> Rises, and I resist,
> Clinging to the steps of the throne.
> Day lifts the darkness from the hills,
> A bright blade cuts the reeds,
> And my life, pitilessly demanding,
> Rises forever in the morning light.

In a poem of this sort, as Jacques Maritain would say, "the conceptual utterances have either disappeared or they are reduced to a minimum or are merely allusive . . . there is no longer any *explicit* intelligible sense, even carried by the images. The intelligible sense drawing in the images is . . . *implicit*."[27] That is to say, if we try to translate into logical prose sense

19

the substance of what we might call the poetic thought (as distinct from rational thought) in this poem, we will come up with very little, for it is inherent in an imagery completely implicated with inward feeling. We can only understand these images by immersing ourselves in their reality. If we do that, allowing imagination to lead us, Louis Simpson's poem takes on new aspects, and we experience them with an intimacy close to bodily sensation. There occurs to us a sense of something like pictorial space in the poem, but it is an interior space we see, an arena of desires, frustrations, fears, and possibilities glimpsed as a barely sketched landscape suffused with "morning light." In keeping with his own conviction that "the deepest image, if it does not move, is only an object,"[28] Simpson sets the poem in motion. The tension between his life's possibilities and demands, associated with the light of day and the indefinite horizon, and the resistance to them, the wish to remain motionless, "clinging to the steps of the throne," increases with the awareness of "rising light." Indeed, the general movement within the space disclosed by the poem is upward—until the gesture of the "bright blade," stroking horizontally across this vertical tendency, severs the poet's "life" like a balloon from its mooring, and, "pitilessly demanding," it ascends eternally into the brightened heavens, presumably drawing him after or at least compelling his undistracted gaze. Having said these things about the poem, we have still hardly touched the suggestiveness of the images and their movements; their sense is "implicit," to repeat Maritain's term, and will be apparent to us only when we place ourselves within the poem's precincts.

There has emerged from the new poetry of dream, surrealism, or pure imagination we have been discussing a new sort of political poem, one which also relies upon an imagery of the subconscious; but now this imagery must reflect something of the buried collective life of the nation, even as Louis Simpson's or W. S. Merwin's poems grow from the submerged areas of their individual lives. Kenneth Patchen's explosive poetry of political and social horror with its juxtapositions of brutality, irrationalism, outraged innocence, and savage satire is a forerunner of more recent work by others; but the chief acknowledged influences are such poets as Whitman, Pasternak, Neruda, and Vallejo. Robert Bly, an eloquent proponent and practitioner of the new political poem, makes some useful remarks in a recent essay, "On Political Poetry," where he stresses the need for poets to "penetrate the husk around their own personalities" and probe the lower regions of the psyche. "Once inside the psyche," Bly maintains, "[they] can speak of inward and political things with the same assurance . . . Paradoxically, what is needed to write true poems about the outward world is inwardness."[29] He wants to divorce such poems from "personal" poems or poems of political "opinions;" however, his very definition of the requirements of inwardness implies that political poems of the kind he favors are at the same time personal as well, for the psyche of the poet has its share in the psyche of the nation.

> The life of the country can be imagined as a psyche larger than the psyche of anyone living, a larger sphere, floating above everyone. In order for the poet to write a true political poem, he has to be able to have such a grasp of his own concerns that he can leave them for a while, and then leap up, like a grasshopper, into this other psyche. In that sphere he finds strange plants and curious many-eyed creatures which he brings back with him. This half-visible psychic life he entangles in his language.[30]

Permitting these statements by Bly to stand without further comment, let us set next to them James Wright's poem "Confession to J. Edgar Hoover," which reveals the poet's almost unbearably intense human concerns, his personal involvement with the material of the poem, coupled with his imaginative

21

capacity for bringing to view levels of existence invisible to the naked eye and unavailable to the reasoning mind. Wright by-passes headlines, news reports, speeches, and platitudes to sound mysterious depths where guilt, alienation, terror, and anxiety that make themselves felt in the outward life of society in other forms have their dark, tentacular roots:

> Hiding in the church of an abandoned stone,
> A Negro soldier
> Is flipping the pages of the Articles of War,
> That he can't read.
> Our father,
> Last evening I devoured the wing
> Of a cloud.
> And, in the city, I sneaked down
> To pray with a sick tree.
> I labor to die, father,
> I ride the great stones,
> I hide under stars and maples,
> And yet I cannot find my own face.
> In the mountains of blast furnaces,
> The trees turn their backs on me.
> Father, the dark moths
> Crouch at the sills of the earth, waiting.
> And I am afraid of my own prayers.
> Father, forgive me.
> I did not know what I was doing.

Departing these twilight regions of the psyche for other areas of consciousness equally tense with disturbance, we are faced with a large, impressive body of writing which has earned in the past few years the title of "confessional" poetry, or as it is called by the British critic A. Alvarez, "Extremist art."[31] While the term confessional is now widely applied, its origin lies in the startling transition that occurred in Robert Lowell's career with the publication of *Life Studies* in 1959. In the decade since that book appeared, Lowell's work has taken on a new surge of power as a result of an unsparing scrutiny of his own life and family, and of an open confrontation with our perilous moment in history. The reader must think at what cost Lowell effected this change in his poetry, a change which recalls exactly Yeats' notion, quoted earlier, of "the re-creation of the man through [his] art."

In his early work Lowell displays considerable rhythmic and imagistic strength which works in the service of a somber, apocalyptic vision of life, growing out of the conflict between his New England heritage and his conversion to Roman Catholicism, and that vision is conveyed as a rule with great rhetorical force in *Lord Weary's Castle* (1946). This style becomes, I think, overworked and heavy-handed in his third book, *The Mills of the Kavanaughs* (1951), and it is a sign of Lowell's poetic intelligence, imagination, and inner resourcefulness that he could remake himself and his art in the years immediately following. *Life Studies* gives us a poetry that seems the living tissue of the man who has written it, for he is never out of sight. As he says in a later poem: "one life, one writing!"

Not only are the new poems of this volume freer, prosier, in style, but they are also unashamedly auto-biographical. They are composed of intimate details, close sketches and glimpses of the poet's parents and grandparents, his friends, several other writers he has known or admired, his wife, and himself. But their most radical and unsettling aspect remains the candid, often frightening revelations of the poet's mental ill-ness and hospitalization in such poems as "Waking in the Blue" and "Skunk Hour." Lowell's admitted interest in the possibilities of prose narrative (which he explores in the autobiographical piece "91 Revere Street," included in *Life Studies*); his liking for the masters of Russian realism, Tolstoy and Chekov, for example; his acquaintance with the poems of his student W. D. Snodgrass which treat the details and crises of private life,[32] all lead toward the transformation of his writing into a manner closer to existence itself and less literary or artificial.

Lowell is extremely frank about himself and his family, though he is perhaps outdone in this respect

23

by Anne Sexton and the late Sylvia Plath. What he says may or may not be true in every respect to the actual lives and personalities of the individuals he portrays, but we cannot be judges of that. What we know are the poems alone. We may object to the use of such private material in poetry, but we will have to prove our objections on the grounds of the poem—that is, whether the use of the material is justified by what is made of it.

To my mind, the poems do justify themselves, for wry and critical or disturbingly self-revealing as some may be, they are conceived in clarity of vision and tempered with compassion and love. If we think of the poems as sketches or studies, not as finished portraits, final and irrevocable, we will see in them the benefits of freedom and informality Lowell is seeking which will permit him to achieve, in his words, "some breakthrough back into life."[33] And these poems are filled with life, its changing moods and order, the pain and pleasure of close relationships, the humor and bittersweetness of remembrance and loss; and through all of these, the sweep of time, the knowledge of death.

The poem "Grandparents," for instance, begins humorously, even flippantly, though that is hardly its main line of feeling. As it proceeds, a few images taken from memories of his adolescence serve to evoke the poet's grandmother and grandfather, and to give their world an impression of remoteness from our own. The first stanza ends by echoing the opening of an elegiac poem by the 17th century English poet Henry Vaughan which starts, "They are all gone into the world of light!/And I alone sit ling'ring here . . ." Then we learn that the poet has inherited his grandparents' farm and now visits it by himself, only to be haunted by recollections of the past. The Vaughan echo actually sounds an alteration in mood as returning memories continue to build up emotional pressure in the poet until he recognizes what we all know intellectually but don't really understand without experiencing its forceful blows upon our deepest affections, our hidden but vital loves: he perceives the irreversible nature of time and events. This realization creates the sudden emotional climax of the poem, which is Lowell's momentary anguished cry of love and need hurled against the inevitable deprivations of life. His emotion released, however, he becomes once more the whimsical, slightly irreverent self we observed at the outset of the poem. His idle doodling with a pencil at the poem's close indicates, in spite of persistent affections, the sharp division that exists between the poet's attitudes and his grandparents' luxurious but trivial mode of living, shut off from the harsher realities of the world and secure in a religiousness that ignored them. The poem compels us to acknowledge the complex ties between past and present in an individual, as well as the wide range of feelings those ties can generate:

> They're altogether otherworldly now,
> those adults champing for their ritual Friday spin
> to pharmacist and five-and-ten in Brockton.
> Back in my throw-away and shaggy span
> of adolescence, Grandpa still waves his stick
> like a policeman;
> Grandmother, like a Mohammedan, still wears her
> thick lavendar mourning and touring veil;
> the Pierce Arrow clears its throat in a horse-stall.
> Then the dry road rises to whiten
> the fatigued elm leaves—
> the nineteenth century, tired of children, is gone.
> They're all gone into a world of light; the farm's
> my own.
> The farm's my own!
> Back there alone,
> I keep indoors, and spoil another season.
> I hear the rattley little country gramophone
> racking its five foot horn:
> "O Summer Time!"
> Even at noon here the formidable
> *Ancien Régime* still keeps nature at a distance. Five
> green shaded light bulbs spider the billiards-table;

no field is greener than its cloth,
where Grandpa, dipping sugar for us both,
once spilled his demitasse.
His favorite ball, the number three,
still hides the coffee stain.
Never again
to walk there, chalk our cues,
insist on shooting for us both.
Grandpa! Have me, hold me, cherish me!
Tears smut my fingers. There
half my life-lease later,
I hold an *Illustrated London News*—;
disloyal still,
I doodle handlebar
mustaches on the last Russian Czar.

Of course, the poems from *Life Studies* which are most unsettling and caused the greatest stir are those dealing with mental breakdown and hospitalization. The title of the poem "Waking in the Blue" refers to the thoughts and sensations that occur to the poet as he wakes early in the morning in a Massachusetts mental hospital. The "azure day" he can see through the window, with its suggestions of freedom and promise, is in biting contrast to his own confined state. Lowell's poem, among other things, records that first moment of waking when we have still a few moments before full consciousness returns and we must face our daily reality, whatever it may happen to be; but the instant of total recollection with which the first stanza concludes is a murderous thrust:

The night attendant, a B. U. Sophomore,
rouses from the mare's-nest of his drowsy head
propped on *The Meaning of Meaning*.
He catwalks down our corridor.
Azure day
makes my agonized blue window bleaker.
Crows maunder on the petrified fairway.
Absence! My heart grows tense
as though a harpoon were sparring for the kill.
(This is the house for the "mentally ill.")

Lowell goes on to describe the wasted lives of the various patients, whose figures merely intensify his sense of restriction, near-hopelessness, and a fear for the future lurks beneath every word. The last stanza combines, in its image of the poet before the mirror, a brief feeling of jauntiness and contentment with the recurrence of quiet desperation over what is yet to be:

> After a hearty New England breakfast,
> I weigh two hundred pounds
> this morning. Cock of the walk,
> I strut in my turtle-necked French sailor's jersey
> before the metal shaving mirrors,
> and see the shaky future grow familiar
> in the pinched, idigenous faces
> of these thoroughbred mental cases,
> twice my age and half my weight.
> We are all old-timers,
> each of us holds a locked razor.

This poem, and "Skunk Hour," which focuses on an agonized moment of mental disorder, are terrible disclosures; in them Lowell takes a more candid, searching look at himself and his situation than most of us would care to, even under reasonably normal conditions. But such pieces spring from a passion born of sheer necessity, and they strike the reader with the force of the poet's life itself. Entering into areas usually marked "Private" in Lowell's work, we do not escape our own existence; rather we find it, and the larger life of our time, reflected there, and in an aspect not too comforting. More recently, Lowell has turned to the public world in some of his poems, though here again he places himself as sensitive, tormented witness to the brutality, ugliness, frightened coldness, and power-craving of America today. "Agonies are one of my changes of garments," Whitman says in *Leaves of Grass,* and Lowell knows only too well the truth of that statement. Four stanzas from another poem of waking, a much later one called "Waking Early Sunday Morning," give us the dilemmas of Lowell the man, conscientious, honest, spiritually bereft, in the midst of a society which has bred them. In a small New England town where Sunday church bells still ring, the poet, now churchless but not irreligious, ponders the

27

fate of belief in an America top heavy with military might and envisages our country's collapse along the lines of an Old Testament precedent:

> O bible chopped and crucified
> in hymns we hear but do not read,
> none of the milder subtleties
> of grace or art will sweeten these
> stiff quatrains shovelled out four-square—
> they sing of peace and preach despair;
> yet they gave darkness some control,
> and left a loophole for the soul.
> No, put old clothes on, and explore
> the corners of the woodshed for
> its dregs and dreck: tools with no handle,
> ten candle-ends not worth a candle,
> old lumber banished from the Temple,
> damned by Paul's precept and example,
> cast from the kingdom, banned in Israel,
> the wordless sign, the tinkling cymbal.
> When will we see Him face to face?
> Each day, He shines through darker glass.
> In this small town where everything
> is known, I see His vanishing
> Emblems, His white spire and flag-
> pole sticking out above the fog,
> like old white china doorknobs, sad,
> slight, useless things to calm the mad.
> Hammering military splendor,
> top-heavy Goliath in full armor—
> little redemption in the mass
> liquidations of their brass,
> elephant and phalanx moving
> with the times and still improving,
> when that kingdom hit the crash:
> a million foreskins stacked like trash . . .

While resorting, as in these stanzas, to formal devices such as rhyming to maintain a certain control, Lowell becomes more elliptical, allusive, and rapid moving. He manages to create the semblance of his own mind's activity as it responds to the experience of contemporary life. Unlike Bly or Wright, who seek to articulate the voices lingering in a dark substratum of collective dreams as the means for comprehending our common condition, Lowell projects himself as a type of representative consciousness, absorbing and suffering the jolts and jars administered from without nd answering them with honesty, directness, and the strength of a gifted, perceptive individual who no onger finds it possible to appeal to an order higher han the human. That spiritual order with which he had some familiarity in the period of his Catholic poems has not vanished entirely but has become clouded, indefinite, its signs as cryptic for him as for the protagonists of Kafka's tales. In Lowell's poetry since *Life Studies*, then, there is the man himself, as A. Alvarez says, "a man of great contradictions, tenderness and violence, a man obsessed equally by his own crack-ups and by the symptoms of crack-up in the society around him."[34]

Similar qualities and obsessions govern a rather considerable body of contemporary poetry, a poetry which, for all the skill, inventiveness, and imagination that go into its composition, still communicates that naked revelation of tormented selfhood seemingly devoid of aesthetic intention. Prufrock's lines, with their implicit pain and frustration, characterize this poetry very well:

> It is impossible to say just what I mean!
> But as if a magic lantern threw the nerves in
> patterns on a screen . . .

The most elaborate work in this canon of confessional or extremist writing is the extensive sequence of John Berryman's *Dream Songs,* which begins with the 77 *Dream Songs* published in 1964 and concludes with the bulky *His Toy, His Dream, His Rest: 308 Dream Songs* that appeared last year. Surely, the impulse for these poems derives from the transformation of Berryman's art initiated by his *Homage to Mistress Bradstreet,* a poem in which the author's voice alternates at times with the imagined voice of the early American poet, and where the tight, elliptic style, with its inverted, idiosyncratic syntax, we encounter in the *Dream Songs* makes its debut. The speaker in all of these frequently untitled pieces is Henry Pussycat,

middle-aged, white, and more and more obviously a
the sequence progresses, a thinly-disguised version o
Berryman himself. But since the poems constitute
stylization of the dreaming mind, there is a constan
shifting back and forth between the first, second, an
third persons to correspond with altering moods
changes in the climate of consciousness; and in addi
tion, Henry occasionally adopts minstrel's black face
talks in Negro dialect, and then is addressed by a
unidentified speaker as Mr. Bones. Curiously, in th
second volume of *Dream Songs,* where the material
of Henry's experience are so obviously those of Berry
man's, and where the work itself is mentioned, the
poet has supplied a prefatory note saying that he i
not to be mistaken for the speaker. Doubtless, a
Lowell notes with respect to *Life Studies,* liberty i
taken with fact, with autobiographical accuracy, fo
the purposes of art; but it is Berryman's consciousnes.
we inhabit, an image of his experience we see throug
the sharp, difficult figure of Henry, and his tormente
spirit of a lapsed Catholic (like Lowell) confronte
with the spectacle of "a sickening century" of war
mass extermination, racial hatred, and power politics
Perhaps the best way of describing the complicate
relationship between poet and speaker is by adoptin,
a line from *Dream Song* #370 to the purpose: "Nake
the man came forth in his mask, to be."

The poems take for themes as a rule the details o
an individual life: loves, marriages, sickness, friend
ship and enmity, poetry, and death; but they mov
outward from these into politics, the sufferings o
others, various manifestations of evil in our time
celebrations and lamentations for several figures—
usually poets Berryman admires and whose loss i
keenly felt: Frost, Roethke, Delmore Schwartz, Loui
MacNeice, R. P. Blackmur, among them. Intermixe
with the toughness, harshness, irrationality, and pain
there are recurrent strains of comedy and of tende

30

lyricism. Underlying the sequence is a gnawing anxiety and guilt, as well as what Berryman calls "an irreversible loss" which Henry has suffered. The latter assumes many forms: the loss of friends, failures of love, the suicide of the poet's father, his collapsed religious convictions, or the terrible nameless dread that can seize him, as in *Dream Song* #29.

> There sat down, once, a thing on Henry's heart
> só heavy, if he had a hundred years
> & more, & weeping, sleepless, in all them time
> Henry could not make good.
> Starts again always in Henry's ears
> the little cough somewhere, an odour, a chime.
>
> And there is another thing he has in mind
> like a grave Sienese face a thousand years
> would fail to blur the still profiled reproach of.
>   Ghastly,
> with open eyes, he attends, blind.
> All the bells say: too late. This is not for tears;
> thinking.
>
> But never did Henry, as he thought he did,
> end anyone and hacks her body up
> and hide the pieces, where they may be found.
> He knows: he went over everyone, & nobody's
>   missing.
> Often he reckons, in the dawn, them up.
> Nobody is ever missing.

Though this sequence explores private associations and the details of personal life, renders the most lucid and the most illogical states of mind, nothing about it is more remarkable than Berryman's combination of formal exactness—each poem (there are a few exceptions) is composed of three six-line stanzas freely rhymed—with bold experiment—he coins words, uses slang, dialect, inverted syntax, and so forth. So no matter how irrational the dream elements may be, they are presented with a precision and tautness of language. Paul Valéry says, "It is the very one who wants to write down his dream who is obliged to be extremely wide awake."[35] In the eighth *Dream Song* Berryman renders the nightmare of the self's destruction by a vicious, anonymous company referred to only as "they;"

yet the grim processes are conveyed in a language that catches the full nature of what is happening without succumbing itself to emotional chaos:

> The weather was fine. They took away his teeth,
> white & helpful; bothered his backhand;
> halved his green hair.
> They blew out his loves, his interests. 'Underneath,'
> (they called in iron voices) 'understand,
> is nothing. So there.'
>
> The weather was very fine. They lifted off
> his covers till he showed, and cringed & pled
> to see himself less.
> They installed mirrors till he flowed. 'Enough'
> (murmured they) 'if you will watch Us instead,
> yet you may saved be. Yes.'
>
> The weather fleured. They weakened all his eyes,
> and burning thumbs into his ears, and shook
> his hand like a notch.
> They flung long silent speeches. (Off the hook!)
> They sandpapered his plumpest hope. (So capsize.)
> They took away his crotch.

"The way is to the destructive element submit yourself," Stein tells Marlowe in Conrad's *Lord Jim*. And many of our contemporary poets are bent on following this course, though the attendant hazards of madness and death loom perliously near for anyone who, through an exposed, vulnerable psyche and nervous system, tries to cross thresholds where the self is strained beyond endurance and shatters. Anne Sexton and Sylvia Plath, two richly-endowed poets, walk such a narrow, dizzying boundary line in their work, sometimes overstepping it; but the price is high—life itself —and Sylvia Plath does not return. The poetry of both these writers rises from the turbulence of private emotions, mental breakdown, spiritual quandaries, and strong attractions to death. To have produced the poems they have given us, charged with beauty and terror, and to have remade themselves as distinctive poetic personalities within those poems by transmuting inner chaos and a compulsion toward death is a moral

32

and artistic triumph for these two women—in spite of Sylvia Plath's tragic suicide.

In "For the Year of the Insane," subtitled "a prayer," Anne Sexton, a confessed "unbeliever," still holds in her hand a "black rosary with its silver Christ" and addresses the Virgin Mary. The theme of her reflective speech is the passage of time, the steady encroachment of age and death, her fear, loneliness, spiritual desolation, and mental instability. No poetry could be more personal:

Closer and closer
comes the hour of my death
as I rearrange my face, grow back,
grow undeveloped and straight-haired.
All this is death.
In the mind there is a thin alley called death
and I move through it as
through water.
My body is useless.
It lies, curled like a dog on the carpet.
It has given up.
There are no words here except the half-learned,
the *Hail Mary* and the *full of grace.*
Now I have entered the year without words.
I note the queer entrance and the exact voltage.
Without words they exist.
Without words one may touch bread
and be handed bread
and make no sound.
O Mary, tender physician,
come with powders and herbs
for I am in the center.
It is very small and the air is gray
as in a steam house.
I am handed wine as a child is handed milk.
It is presented in a delicate glass
with a round bowl and a thin lip.
The wine itself is pitch-colored, musty and secret.
The glass rises on its own toward my mouth
and I notice this and understand this
only because it has happened.
I have this fear of coughing
but I do not speak,
a fear of rain, a fear of the horseman
who comes riding into my mouth.
The glass tilts on its own
and I am on fire.

I see two thin streaks burn down my chin.
I see myself as one would see another.
I have been cut in two.
O Mary, open your eyelids.
I am in the domain of silence,
the kingdom of the crazy and the sleeper.
There is blood here
and I have eaten it.
O mother of the womb,
did I come for blood alone?
O little mother,
I am in my own mind.
I am locked in the wrong house.

The experience Anne Sexton renders may remind us by its intense, visionary qualities, of the drama of Roethke's "In a Dark Time." Though the poem strikes into the most private domains and alternates between self-examination, supplication, and a hallucination that approaches madness yet is also strangely ritual and sacramental, the consciousness of the poet becomes a reflection of the spiritual unrest and tension in which many of us may share and the terrible frustration we feel at being trapped by the limited perspective of our own egos. And the same may be said for Sylvia Plath, particularly with respect to the poems of her final collection, *Ariel,* where her own "controlled hallucination," as Robert Lowell calls it in his foreword to the book, and the poetic powers freed by her neuropathic state permit her entry into the most extreme conditions of awareness and feeling. The poems are filled with motion, relentless energy, abrupt, shifting imagery, and the expanding, altering identity of the poet herself. In "Getting There," for instance, conceiving herself involved in "some war or other," she is moving in a train across Russia through a veritable hell of death, destruction, and brutality; the images follow one another in rapid succession with the poet both seeing and participating in what occurs. At the conclusion of the poem she survives miraculously and is reborn. If the experience seems confused, disordered, that is Miss Plath's intention and not the failures of the neurotic;

34

for no matter what perceptions and hallucinatory visions her mental states made available, these are worked with consummate, determined skill and craft into her poems. As she remarks in an interview not long before her death:

> . . . I must say I cannot sympathize with these cries from the heart that are informed by nothing except a needle or a knife, or whatever it is. I believe that one should be able to control and manipulate experiences, even the most terrifying, like madness, being tortured, this sort of experience, and one should be able to manipulate these experiences with an informed and an intelligent mind. I think that personal experience is very important, but certainly it shouldn't be a kind of shut-box and mirror-looking, narcissistic experience. I believe it should be *relevant,* and relevant to the larger things, the bigger things such as Hiroshima and Dachau and so on.[36]

So the nervous and emotional illness which assails her inner life for Miss Plath becomes a means whereby she can gain access to experience not outwardly hers; the liberated imagination takes on the life of others. This kind of identification takes place in "Getting There"; here is the last half of the poem:

> How far is it?
> There is mud on my feet,
> Thick, red and slipping. It is Adam's side,
> This earth I cannot rise from, and I in agony.
> I cannot undo myself, and the train is steaming.
> Steaming and breathing, its teeth
> Ready to roll, like a devil's.
> There is a minute at the end of it
> A minute, a dewdrop.
> How far is it?
> It is so small
> The place I am getting to, why are there these
>   Obstacles—
> The body of this woman,
> Charred skirts and deathmask
> Mourned by religious figures, by garlanded children.
> And now detonations—
> Thunder and guns.
> The fire's between us.
> Is there no still place
> Turning and turning in the middle air,
> Untouched and untouchable.

The train is dragging itself, it is screaming—
An animal
Insane for the destination,
The bloodspot,
The face at the end of the flare.
I shall bury the wounded like pupas,
I shall count and bury the dead.
Let their souls writhe in a dew,
Incense in my track.
The carriages rock, they are cradles.
And I, stepping from this skin
Of old bandages, boredoms, old faces
Step to you from the black car of Lethe,
Pure as a baby.

In the last turning this survey of various manifestations of the personal element among contemporary poets will take, I want to cite the work of a few poets who have, in their individual manner, followed the leads suggested both in theory and in practice by William Carlos Williams—and by Ezra Pound, H. D., and, to a certain extent, Kenneth Rexroth as well. A number of these poets are called the Black Mountain group, after Black Mountain College, where many of them first met and began to formulate their notions of poetry; or they are called Projectivists, after Charles Olson's influential essay on "Projective Verse." What links them together, beyond friendships and apparently a great amount of literary correspondence, is less a close similarity of poetic practice than the acceptance of Williams and the other poets mentioned as their guides and mentors. As Denise Levertov writes in "September 1961," a moving tribute to Pound, Williams, and H. D.:

They have told us
the road leads to the sea,
and given
the language into our hands.

Williams in his essays urges the abandonment of the iambic pentameter, the sonnet form, and other English poetic conventions that he strongly believes prevent America from producing its own contemporary poetry, a poetry deriving from American speech and its rhythms, developing a new and relative kind of "measure," to use his favorite term, in opposition to the fixed poetic foot. But, more than that, in his poems and his prose, there is a concentrated attention to particulars, to immediate environment, to objects in all their detailed concreteness, which thus defines the self that perceives. Williams notes in the introduction to a book of his poems, *The Wedge:*

> When a man makes a poem, makes it, mind you, he takes words as he finds them interrelated about him and composes them—without distortion which would mar their exact significances—into an intense expression of his perceptions and ardors that they may constitute a revelation in the speech that he uses. It isn't what he *says* that counts as a work of art, it's what he makes, with such intensity of perception that it lives with an intrinsic movement of its own to verify its authenticity.[37]

In the work of Denise Levertov, Robert Creeley, Gary Snyder, Larry Eigner, Robert Duncan, Charles Olson, and Paul Blackburn, among others, we discover the poetic realization of the process Williams describes. The poet's focus is frequently on his life as a person: his daily encounters with *things,* with others; the character of his relationships, even the most intimate ones; the movements of his thought and sensation; the nature of his interior being as it emerges in dream or vision. Yet personal as this poetry is, it can never be mistaken for the writing of the confessional poets: for while it does not avoid the harsh actualities of present-day existence nor painful areas of private experience, it also does not evidence much interest in psychic disturbance, emotional and spiritual torment, the sense of victimization, and emotional pressures that threaten to explode into madness. For the poets I have named the act of poetry—and all of them, I believe, are fascinated with the process of composition itself—is a matter of the most profound significance to the individual, because it is through that act that he fashions his own single identity—becoming a proper human being and making a poem properly are two sides of the same endeavor. In Charles Olson's words:

> . . . a man, carved
> out of himself, so wrought he
> fills his given space, makes
> traceries sufficient to
> others' needs . . .[38]

And Denise Levertov, who quotes this statement by Olson, has a remark of her own which, together with Olson's, brings out the double emphasis of their poetics: the stress on the fulfillment of the poet's self and on the poem as directed to readers. Miss Levertov says: "The act of realizing inner experience in material substance is in itself an action *towards others,* even when the conscious intention has not gone beyond the desire for self-expression."[39]

In Denise Levertov's poems or Robert Creeley's or Robert Duncan's there is an impression given to the reader of having stepped into a new kind of space, an invisible but nonetheless real zone bounded by the interlocking form of words yet receiving its substance from the felt presence of the poet. This space is, in correspondence with Charles Olson's views, an aspect of the poet's being, a part of his life. Admittedly, what I am saying may seem difficult, hard to understand clearly, but it can be grasped more readily through the experience of the poetry. Or we may think of how our bodies create what we might call their own singular space around themselves as we perform all the gestures and activities of living. It is that sense of presence, involving the total self of the writer, physical and spiritual, that reaches us in the work of these poets.

Again, I shall offer a couple of examples, wishing I could be more comprehensive. The last section of Denise Levertov's poem "The Coming Fall" blends description of an external setting with the gradual effects of that situation as it is felt inwardly by the poet herself, coming first through bodily sensations:

38

> Down by the fallen fruit in the old orchard
> the air grows cold. The hill
> hides the sun.
> A sense of the present
> rises out of earth and grass,
> enters the feet, ascends
> into the genitals, constricting
> the breast, lightening
> the head—a wisdom,
> a shiver, a delight
> that what is passing
> is here, as if
> a snake went by, green in the
> gray leaves.

Here the "sense of the present," an evanescent trace of feeling and physical sensation which would normally elude words, is beautifully caught; and it remains true to its origins, for there is no attempt to put intellectual constructions upon it. Miss Levertov tries to return us, through the poem, to the moment of the experience itself. In her poem "A Common Ground" she tells us how, ideally, poetry should so transform reality that in perceiving the elements that comprise our world, in carrying out the tasks and necessities of daily life, we would be absorbing poetry:

> Poems stirred
> into paper coffee-cups, eaten
> with petals on rye in the
> sun—the cold shadows in back,
> and the traffic grinding the
> borders of spring—entering
> human lives forever,
> unobserved, a spring element . . .

Miss Levertov's search, as she says in "Matins," is for "the authentic," which appears both in dreams, the inward life, and in waking actualities; it is "the known/appearing fully itself, and/more itself than one knew." In discovering this true nature and abundance of known reality, the poet formulates her—and our— solidarity, human community, with it.

Gary Snyder's poetry, some of the finest of recent years, draws on his experiences of camping and mountain-climbing, working in logging camps in the forests of the Pacific Northwest, laboring as a tanker hand, studying the life and lore of American Indians, and, finally, spending years in Japan studying under a Zen master in Kyoto. In certain poems from his book *Riprap* (1959) he gives a sense of the immensity of the wilderness, of non-human nature, of its seemingly eternal, mute history, against which human activity, culture, and consciousness appear insignificant. By his control of rhythm and language, his accuracy of detail, he resists being overwhelmed; and the poem, in turn, recreating the man and his experience, humanizes it, if you will. The recognition is no less disturbing but has been assimilated to consciousness, made part of our awareness of reality; or to repeat Denise Levertov's words, "the known/appearing fully itself, and/more itself than one knew." One such poem of Gary Snyder's is "Above Pate Valley":

> We finished clearing the last
> Section of trail by noon,
> High on the ridge-side
> Two thousand feet above the creek—
> Reached the pass, went on
> Beyond the white pine groves,
> Granite shoulders, to a small
> Green meadow watered by the snow,
> Edged with Aspen—sun
> Straight high and blazing
> But the air was cool.
> Ate a cold fried trout in the
> Trembling shadows. I spied
> A glitter, and found a flake
> Black volcanic glass—obsidian—
> By a flower. Hands and knees
> Pushing the Bear grass, thousands
> Of arrowhead leavings over a
> Hundred yards. Not one good
> Head, just razor flakes
> On a hill snowed all but summer,
> A land of fat summer deer,
> They came to camp. On their
> Own trails. I followed my own
> Trail here. Picked up the cold-drill,
> Pick, singlejack, and sack
> Of dynamite.
> Ten thousand years.

Something of the enormous range and vitality of current American poetry has, I hope, impressed itself in the course of these remarks, which I intended to distinguish the pronounced personal qualities evident among contemporary poets of the last three or so decades and also to provide a partial survey of the different kinds of writers and writing involved. I have avoided, as I said I would, any attempt at very close definition; that should come later, as the job of the sympathetic, imaginative literary historian. Instead, I have tried to be suggestive and illustrative, and to keep before you examples of the poetry itself, since it is, after all, more important than anything that might be said about it. There are many other poets whom I would have liked to introduce here, but such an attempt is impracticable; so I confined myself to three prominent tendencies for the purposes at hand. Within the landscape of contemporary poetry, as I believe my choices demonstrated, there are a number of talented writers, and their styles, their notions of what a poem ought to be or do, diverge widely. Yet it is not too much to say that they have in common a concern for experience which lies nearest them, within the radius of their actual lives: the space—to return to that metaphor—outside themselves, through which they move, in which they act and meet others, or the space within, the inward world of dream, vision, and meditation. This concern enables them to combat those abstracting, tabulating, depersonalizing forces our society produces by asserting through poems the value of their unique human nature and experience. Once again, Denise Levertov helps us; she writes of the stages of awareness leading up to poetic activity: "The progression seems clear to me: from Reverence for Life to Attention to Life, from Attention to Life to a highly developed Seeing and Hearing, from Seeing and Hearing (faculties almost indistinguishable for the poet) to the Discovery and Revelation of Form, from Form to Song."[40] A similar process, however unconscious of it the poet may be, however it might differ in certain particulars, appears to me to govern the work of those poets we have discussed. I can say little more for my part now except that the burden of the proof is in the reading of our contemporaries, and that careful attention from the reader will be repaid by an encounter with poems bold and various in form, attitude, and insight; poems which, like the poets we discover within them, are unimpeachable in their integrity, intense in their vision. In Yeats' pregnant phrase, "creation's very self" is what we look for, and find. Denise Levertov, in the third of her "Three Meditations," offers us an image of the poet's activity with which I should like to leave you in mind:

> We breathe an ill wind,
> nevertheless our kind
> in mushroom multitudes
> jostles for elbow-room
> moonwards
>
> an equalization of
> hazards
> bringing the poet
> back to song
> as before
>
> to sing of death
> as before
> and life, while he
> has it, energy
>
> being in him a singing,
> a beating of gongs, efficacious
> to drive away devils,
> response to
>
> the wonder that
> as before
> shows a double face,
>
> to be
> what he is
> being his virtue
>
> filling his whole space
> so no devil
> may enter.

Ralph J. Mills, Jr.

42

REFERENCES

[1] Charles Olson: "Projective Verse," in *Human Universe and Other Essays*, edited by Donald M. Allen (New York, 1967), p. 54.

[2] Randall Jarrell: "The End of the Line," in *Literary Opinion in America*, edited by M. D. Zabel (New York, 1951), p. 747.

[3] *Contemporary American Poetry*, edited by Donald Hall (Baltimore, 1962), p. 17.

[4] James Dickey: *The Suspect in Poetry* (Madison, Minn., 1964), pp. 55-56.

[5] T. S. Eliot: *Selected Essays 1917-1932* (New York, 1932), pp. 8; 7.

[6] Louis Simpson: "Dead Horses and Live Issues," *The Nation* (April 24, 1967), p. 520.

[7] *The Autobiography of William Butler Yeats* (New York, 1958), p. 183.

[8] Introduction to *The New Writing in the U.S.A.*, edited by Donald Allen and Robert Creeley (Harmondsworth, Middlesex, 1967), p. 18.

[9] Ortega y Gassett: *The Dehumanization of Art and Other Essays* (New York, 1956), p. 175.

[10] Martin Buber: *I and Thou*, translated by R. G. Smith (New York, 1958), pp. 11; 10.

[11] Kenneth Rexroth: *Bird in the Bush: Obvious Essays* (New York, 1959), p. 12.

[12] Denise Levertov: "Origins of a Poem," *Michigan Quarterly Review* (Fall, 1968), p. 238.

[13] "On Identity," in *On the Poet and His Craft: Selected Prose of Theodore Roethke*, edited by Ralph J. Mills, Jr. (Seattle, 1965), p. 21.

[14] An illuminating account of these years is to be found in Allan Seager: *The Glass House: The Life of Theodore Roethke* (New York, 1968).

[15] "Open Letter," in *On the Poet and His Craft*, p. 41.

[16] For discussions, see *The Contemporary Poet as Artist and Critic*, edited by Anthony Ostroff (Boston, 1964); Karl Malkoff: *Theodore Roethke* (New York, 1966); *Theodore Roethke: Essays on the Poetry*, edited by Arnold Stein (Seattle, 1965).

[17] *The Contemporary Poet as Artist and Critic*, p. 49.

[18] Preface to St.-John Perse: *Anabasis*, translated by T. S. Eliot (New York, 1949), p. 10.

[19] From "I Cry, Love! Love!" in *Collected Poems of Theodore Roethke* (New York, 1966), p. 92.

[20] *The Distinctive Voice*, edited by William J. Martz (Glenview, Ill., 1966), p. 247.

[21] *The Nation* (April 24, 1967), p. 521.

[22] *Mid-Century French Poets*, edited by Wallace Fowlie (New York, 1955), p. 175.

[23] Louis Simpson in *The Distinctive Voice*, p. 247.

[24] *The New American Painting* (New York, 1959), p. 64.

25*The New American Poetry 1945-1960,* edited by Donald M. Allen (New York, 1960), p. 419.

26*The Distinctive Voice,* pp. 269-270.

27Jacques Maritain: *Creative Intuition in Art and Poetry* (New York, 1955), p. 197.

28*The Distinctive Voice,* p. 247.

29Robert Bly: "On Political Poetry," *The Nation* (April 24, 1967), p. 522.

30Ibid., p. 522.

31See A. Alvarez: *Beyond All This Fiddle* (London, 1968); also on confessional poetry, M. L. Rosenthal: *The New Poets* (New York, 1967).

32See Frederick Seidel's interview with Lowell, in *Robert Lowell: A Collection of Critical Essays,* edited by Thomas Parkinson (Englewood Cliffs, N.J., 1968).

33*Robert Lowell: A Collection of Critical Essays,* p. 19.

34A. Alvarez: *Beyond All This Fiddle,* p. 14.

35Paul Valery: *The Art of Poetry,* translated by Denise Folliot (New York, 1958), p. 11.

36*The Poet Speaks,* edited by Peter Orr (London, 1966), pp. 169-170.

37*Selected Essays of William Carlos Williams* (New York, 1954), p. 257.

38Quoted by Denise Levertov, *Michigan Quarterly Review* (Fall 1968), p. 236.

39Ibid., p. 235.

40*Michigan Quarterly Review* (Fall 1968), p. 238.